Windsurfing

Windsurfing

An Introduction to Boardsailing

Diana C. Gleasner

Photographs by Bill Gleasner

ICS BOOKS, INC.
MERRILLVILLE, INDIANA

WINDSURFING

Published by:
ICS Books, Inc.
1000 E. 80th Place
Merrillville, IN 46410

Distributed by:
Stackpole Books
Cameron and Kelker Street
Harrisburg, PA 17105

Library of Congress Cataloging in Publication Data

Gleasner, Diana C.
    Windsurfing : an introduction to boardsailing.

    1. Windsurfing   I. Title.
GV811.63.W56G57   1985   797.1'72   85-14275
ISBN 0-934802-24-6

ABOUT THE AUTHOR

Diana Gleasner was born in New Jersey and earned her B.A. at Ohio Wesleyan University and her M.A. at the University of Buffalo. She was a high school teacher for about six years but now devotes full time to writing. Besides magazine articles she has written 25 books. She enjoys swimming, waterskiing and canoeing.

Diana is married to Bill Gleasner who supplied most of the photographs for WINDSURFING. He is a full-time free lance photographer and together they make a fine photo-journalism team as this book demonstrates.

The Gleasners live in North Carolina and travel extensively in North America. They have recently spent time in Hawaii where Bill took the photographs for WINDSURFING.

Windsurfing is a sport that takes its name from the registered trademark name Windsurfer® used by Windsurfing International, Incorporated for its product. The word Windsurfer® is a trademark. We have omitted the trademark designation throughout the text of this book to make it easier for young people to read and in no way indicates the word Windsurfer® is not under trademark protection.

Photograph facing page 1 and on page 48 courtesy of Windsurfing International.

The author wishes to thank Ranney Warburton, Chris O'Leary, Lunnar Wickman and Chompers (canine boardsailor of the first order) of the International Windsurfing Academy of Kalapaki Beach, Kauai, Hawaii, and Peter Webber of Westport Country Club, Denver, North Carolina.

**For my brother, Bud,
also known as Edward S. Cottle,
with memories of skimming across
Nawiliwili Bay.**

TABLE OF CONTENTS

CHAPTER ONE

WHY?

With the sun on your back and the water riffling around your toes, you grab the wind in your hands. You lean back, pick up speed and your craft becomes a part of you. Windsurfing demands total involvement, but the pay-off is high adventure. This is the purest form of sailing and by far the most fun.

At first everyone feels awkward. You'll probably spend more time climbing back on board than sailing, but you'll soon be skimming over the water. Be patient; it's not hard to learn. A couple of afternoons should do it.

One of the best things about windsurfing is that it's simple. It takes less than five minutes to put together the rig. It's easy to transport and store. You won't have to wait in line, find a partner or stop at a gas pump. All you need are water and wind, and within moments you've escaped the world of traffic lights.

You can enjoy windsurfing whether you're a beginner or an old hand, in light puffy winds or in heavy seas. With wet suits, even cool weather is fine for windsurfing.

Windsurfing is safe. The water and sail cushion your falls. The board will always float, even if you take a buzz saw to it. It

won't run away from you since the sail holds the board in place like a sea anchor. Anyone with common sense will find it hard to get into trouble.

Once you've paid for the sailboard and have found some water, the sport is very cheap. Upkeep is low. There are no mooring fees or yacht club dues. The wind is free.

Best of all, you'll never be bored. There's always something new to learn. Once you can lean backward and dunk your head while underway, you're ready for some more demanding acrobatics. You say you can actually soar off a steep wave using your sail for a wing? Maybe you're ready for competition. Regattas are held wherever there are board sailors. Once you've proven yourself a winner on the local circuit, you can go for the gold. Windsurfing is now officially an Olympic sport.

Challenges? In windsurfing they stretch as far as the horizon.

CHAPTER TWO

HISTORY

Wouldn't it be great, Hoyle Schweitzer said, if surfing were more like sailing? Surfers waste so much time waiting for the right kind of waves. Then when the surf is finally up, it's often too crowded to be fun. Sailing doesn't demand such exact conditions. Besides, sailors can use the whole ocean instead of just the small area near the shore. They definitely have an advantage.

Hoyle's friend, Jim Drake, disagreed. He thought surfers were more fortunate. In just a short time, they can run to the water, toss in the board and start riding the waves. At least they don't spend good time rigging the boat and then putting everything back when they're through. If Jim has only an hour, he doesn't even bother taking his boat out. He knows he'll have too little time to actually sail.

Schweitzer and Drake decided what they really needed was a combination of the two -- a sailing surfboard. It sounded like a crazy idea at first. Both men were creative thinkers, used to solving new and challenging problems. Schweitzer was vice president of a computer firm. Drake was an aeronautical engineer.

Drake had been exchanging new sailing ideas with one of his

scientist friends, Fred Payne, for years. Schweitzer and Drake began to design a craft that would combine the best of sailing with the best of surfing. A number of ideas were tried and thrown out. In 1967 the two Californians tried an enlarged surfboard. The tricky part was finding a way to steer it without a rudder. A universal joint which let the sail move freely in all directions and a wishbone boom controlled by a standing sailor brought about an entirely new way of sailing. They called it the "free sail system."

The original sailboards were, like surfboards, made of fiberglass. A lighter, longer lasting and less expensive material was needed. The answer was polyethylene, the same plastic used in making frisbees.

In 1969 Jim Drake presented a paper to the American Institute for Aeronautics and Astronauctics on "Wind Surfing -- A New Concept in Sailing." It wasn't long before experts were agreeing it was the first really original sailing idea in 100 years.

Hoyle Schweitzer, after making a few sailboards for his friends, quit his job with the computer firm and set up shop in his garage. Interest was high from the beginning. A man driving by saw a Windsurfer off Malibu, ran down to the beach in his business suit and ordered six of "whatever they were" on the spot. **Dupont** magazine ran a cover story on windsurfing which resulted in a flood of orders.

Hoyle and Diane Schweitzer closed their living-room office and moved the business to larger quarters. Soon they needed even more room and moved to a large plant in Marina del Ray.

Europeans immediately took to the small size and high performance of the Windsurfers. A dry land simulator was invented which made it possible to teach the basics on shore. Soon the first windsurfing schools were opened in Sweden and Germany.

By 1980 Windsurfing International was a multi-million dollar business. Dealers had sprung up around the world, and certified International Windsurfer Sailing Schools were teaching eager beginners the marvels of sailing on a surfboard.

CHAPTER THREE

EQUIPMENT AND ITS CARE

The sailboard has been kept as simple and basic as possible. Its parts are easy to handle and maintain. A few pointers on care will help you get the most pleasure from your craft.

The board weighs about 40 pounds. It can easily be carried by one person. The standard size is approximately 12 feet by 2 feet, slightly longer than a surfboard. Wider models offer more stability for learners. Most experts prefer the rocket, which has foot straps for greater control at high speeds. The inner core is polyurethane foam which provides stiffness as well as buoyancy. The outer shell is made of the same kind of plastic as a frisbee (polyethylene). This long-lasting material is not affected by warmth, cold or salt water. It can be kept clean by an occasional soap washing. To keep the standing area in the mid-section of the board from becoming slippery, apply beeswax or wax aerosol from time to time.

The skeg is a small fixed fin on the underside of the stern which makes the board more stable. Without the skeg, the board would be difficult to steer because it would slide sideways. When

you leave your board on the beach or shore, turn it upside down. Otherwise, someone may be tempted to jump on it and might break the skeg.

The daggerboard, which juts down through a slot in the center, keeps the board moving straight ahead. It's made of plastic, fiberglass or wood. It should fit snugly but still be lifted easily by pulling on the daggerboard strap with one hand. When sailing into shore or shallow water, be sure to pull the daggerboard up so you don't damage it when you run aground.

The rig consists of the mast, boom and sail. If you take the mast apart, you'll find it has three separate pieces: a short round wooden plug called the mast tip, the mast itself and a universal joint at the lower end. The flexible pole is made of fiberglass-reinforced plastic or aluminum and is about 13 feet, 9 inches long. Be very careful not to bump the ends of the mast when storing or transporting it.

The universal joint connects the mast to the board. No other sailing craft has this feature. That's the reason none of them can be used in as many different ways as a sailboard. The universal joint makes it possible for the mast and sail to lie flat in the water or to tilt and turn in any direction. It lets the boardsailor tack and jibe easily and accurately.

The wishbone boom, with the help of the mast, keeps the sail extended. You raise the sail by pulling on the uphaul line, then grasp the boom to control the sailboard. Made of laminated teak or alloy, the boom is your support and your way of steering.

The standard board sail is 56 square feet. Larger sails are used for racing or in light breezes and smaller storm sails are available for strong wind conditions. Clear plastic windows make it possible to see in all directions when sailing. Except for the sleeve which is pulled over the mast, the triangular sail is the same as sails used by conventional boats. It is usually made of Dacron or some other lightweight synthetic fiber that doesn't rot.

A board sail gets much rougher treatment than a boat sail because it's constantly being dropped into the water. Take a few extra minutes to give it proper care. Spread it out to dry and shake off any sand before putting it away. Inspect your sail regularly for signs of wear, particularly around the seams. Make temporary repairs on the spot with adhesive tape. When you get home sew the rip right away with a needle and terylene thread so it doesn't tear more the next time you sail. The sail will keep its shape better if you fold it carefully before stowing it in the sail bag. Don't bend the plastic windows too sharply -- they might crack.

CHAPTER FOUR

CLOTHING

If the water temperature is over 68°F and the air above 75°F, a swim suit will probably be all the clothing you'll need. If you want to be comfortable in cooler water, you'll need a wet suit.

A lot of body heat is lost in this sport because of the constant evaporation of spray. Long sessions on the board in chilly weather can lead to exposure. This is known as hypothermia. This chilling of the body's core can be fatal. It strikes without much warning and can affect your ability to make wise decisions. A good wet suit for protection is your best bet. Even a thin, partial suit is helpful.

Most wet suits are made of foam neoprene protected by nylon fabric inside and out. They trap a thin film of water next to your skin. This water is then heated by your body. The suit should be snug. If it's too tight you won't be able to move freely. Be sure you can kneel comfortably and stretch your legs easily. The best suits are soft and stretchy.

Boardsailors wear a thinner suit than divers, usually 3 to 6 mm. thick. If the outfit is too heavy, it saps your energy. Remember a wet suit is buoyant. While it won't support an unconscious person, it **will** help you stay afloat.

If you feel chilly and don't have a wet suit, you may be tempted to wear a t-shirt. Don't. You'll be colder than with bare skin because the water will keep evaporating from the shirt. Try warding off the spray by wearing a lightweight windbreaker. This will slow down evaporation and you'll stay warmer. Also, windbreakers are water resistant and dry quickly. It should be loose enough so you can move freely. One with snaps rather than a zipper is less likely to fill up with air each time you fall.

In cool weather, protection for your hands may help your grip. Some sailors prefer waterskier's gloves made of thin rubberized cloth. Others buy inexpensive household rubber gloves. Diver's neoprene gloves are so thick your hands will tire quickly. If you do buy them for very cold days be sure to get the ones with the chamois leather palms for a better grip.

Shoes are excellent for protection or warmth or both. They can help you avoid minor injuries from the hardware on the board as well as from rocks and debris. There's no sense worrying about coral, sea urchins or trash in the water. Choose shoes that are flexible and easy to put on and take off. Some sailors prefer boat shoes, others use tennis shoes. For raw days, tennis shoes over neoprene socks are best.

CHAPTER FIVE

WHEN AND WHERE TO LEARN

You can teach yourself to windsurf, but it's easier and more fun if you join a class. A warm day with a very light breeze and a small calm body of water are the best conditions for learning. A pond or bay with gently sloping sandy beaches is ideal. Avoid powerboat wakes, crowded areas, strong currents and rocky shorelines.

Dead calm conditions won't work well. You need some pressure on the sail for balance and to get moving. Choose a day with a steady 3 to 6 knot wind, certainly no more than Force 3 on the Beaufort Wind Scale. Force 2 winds are better, especially if you're learning with a standard 56 square foot sail.

Beaufort Wind Scale

Force 1 - (1-3 knot wind) light air, smooth or slightly rippled water

Force 2 - (4-6 knot wind) light breeze, rippled water

Force 3 - (7-l0 knot wind) gentle breeze, large wavelets

An onshore breeze (one that blows you back toward shore) or a breeze that is parallel to the shore will be helpful. Beginners tend to be carried with the wind. If you're not skilled at tacking back against the wind, you can get yourself into big trouble with an offshore breeze. It may blow you so far out that the paddle back is exhausting and dangerous.

Lightning and strong, gusty winds that usually go with thunder storms are dangerous. Head for shore at the first sign of a storm. Never leave your board. It's your life raft. In an emergency give the international distress signal -- repeatedly raise and lower your arms over your head.

CHAPTER SIX

LEARNING ON LAND

You can speed up your learning by practicing the basics of windsurfing on land. A simulator, used by most windsurfing schools, will cut your confusion way down.

This is a sailboard or the standing area of a board mounted on springs. Because it turns and tilts in all directions and acts much like a sailboard on the water, a simulator will help you learn the basics and get the feel of the wind in the sail. When you lose your balance, just jump down. This is far less tiring and not nearly as discouraging as having to crawl back on the board from deep water over and over again. Also, an instructor can stand by and correct your mistakes right away.

If you don't have an instructor and a simulator, you'll still be better off starting on land. You won't need the board, just the rig -- the sail, boom and mast. Dig a small hole in the ground or the sand for the mast foot. This will take the place of the slot the mast foot fits into on the board.

Lay the sail on the ground so the foot of the mast points toward the direction from which the wind is coming. The top of the mast should point in the direction to which it is blowing. Stand with

your back to the wind. Place the mast foot between your feet and pretend the front of the board is to your right. Grab the uphaul rope with both hands and raise the sail until the boom is off the ground. The mast will be almost straight and the sail will be fluttering in the wind. Holding the uphaul line with elbows bent, gently swing the rig to get the feel of it. Take your right hand off the uphaul, cross it over the hand holding the rope and grasp the boom about five inches from the mast. Now let go of the uphaul rope with your left hand and balance the rig with your right hand only. Pull the mast forward past your right shoulder. Catch hold of the boom with your left hand. Pull it in slowly until it just begins to fill with wind. The mast should be upright and slightly tilted toward the forward end of the board.

When the pressure increases so much that you feel yourself being pulled onto the falling sail, let the left hand go. Beginners tend to drop the mast hand (right hand in this case) by mistake. When you let the left arm out, the wind doesn't fill the entire sail which makes it much easier to hold. Practice these steps until you can raise the sail and "get underway" without thinking through each step.

CHAPTER SEVEN

CARRYING AND LAUNCHING

If you have to take your sailboard more than a short distance, it's easier to carry the rig and the board separately. Leave the sail rolled around the mast and the boom folded up against it. Carry the board under one arm with your hand in the daggerboard slot. Some people prefer to insert the daggerboard for a better handhold. Others carry the board with one hand in the mast step slot and the other in the daggerboard slot. Carry the rig above your head by holding the boom in one hand and the mast in the other. If the length of the mast is pointed toward the wind, the breeze lifts the sail making it lighter to carry. When you reach the water, unfurl the sail.

You may want to drag your craft fully rigged and ready to go if the distance is not too far. Stand between the mast and the board with the nose of the board under one arm, the sail uphaul in the other hand. Try not to scratch the equipment on rough surfaces.

Place or throw the sail onto the water first. It'll stay where you put it even in strong winds. The board will drift away much faster. Be sure the water is deep enough so the daggerboard doesn't bump on the bottom. Insert the daggerboard with its point toward

the rear of the hull and climb on. Paddle the board to the floating sail, plug the universal joint into the slot on the board and grab the unphaul line. You're in business.

BALANCING

Balance is far more important than strength in windsurfing. Before you try raising the sail, get used to the motion of the floating board. Climb up on the sailboard near the daggerboard, turn and sit with both feet in the water. Next, kneel astride the daggerboard, turn and sit with both feet in the water. Next, kneel astride the daggerboard slot holding onto the sides of the board. Tilt the board from side to side to get the feel of it. Stand up slowly, keeping your weight over the centerline. Stay as relaxed as possible. Try turning in a circle, first in one direction, then in the other. You'll be glad to know that the addition of the daggerboard and the sail will make the sailboard much more stable.

PADDLING

Every boardsailor should know the best ways to paddle for convenience as well as safety. If the water is calm, the breeze light and you don't have far to go, lay the boom on the back of the board to keep mast and sail from dragging in the water. Paddle with your hands while kneeling or lying on the board. You can also sit facing backward and hold the sail in place with one hand while you paddle with the other. If you just want to stop drifting, leave the sail in the water. It makes a great sea anchor.

If you're in waves or strong wind, take the rig apart. Carefully roll the sail and tie it firmly to the mast. Place all the parts lengthwise along the center of the board, kneel or lie on them and paddle. Be sure nothing is trailing in the water. If the distance is short, it does not matter whether you leave the daggerboard in the slot or not. To move faster you might need to use the daggerboard or the mast (without sail and booms) as a paddle.

If the parts of your sailboard become separated, remember a rigged sail will stay in place but a board will quickly drift away. **Go after the board and don't leave it.** It is a life raft which will keep you afloat indefinitely. You'll stay warmer and the white board will be easier to spot than you would be if you were in the water. Besides, you can paddle faster and farther than you can swim.

It pays to practice paddling in calm water. Learning to paddle in the middle of a squall is not a good idea.

CHAPTER EIGHT

CLIMBING ABOARD
and
LIFTING THE SAIL
FROM THE WATER

Climb onto the board near the daggerboard slot from the windward side. While kneeling grab the uphaul line of the sail which is lying on top of the water. You may have to swing the mast in next to the board in order to reach the uphaul easily. Once you have hold of the line, move the mast so that it's at right angles to the board. Your back should be to the wind and your feet on the board's centerline on either side of the mast.

Now you want to pull the rig (mast, boom and sail) slowly out of the water. Squat with your back straight as you lift the sail just enough to let the water run off it. If you are bent over with your bottom sticking out, you'll be pulled off balance when the sail clears the water. Slowly straighten your legs, leaning slightly backward.

If you begin to fall, let the uphaul line slide through your hands until you get your balance back. Then begin raising the mast again, letting one hand go to steady yourself if you need to.

The most important thing to remember is to always keep your mast at right angles to the board. Wait for the breeze to catch the sail and turn it downwind. Bring the line in until the boom is completely out of the water. Let the sail flutter while you hold the uphaul as close to the boom as possible. Tilt the mast forward or backward to keep the sail downwind and pull the rig toward you until you feel almost no tension. The mast should stay upright over the universal joint with very little effort. Don't take your hands off the uphaul until you're completely balanced. You are now ready to get underway.

CHAPTER NINE

GETTING UNDERWAY
and
SAILING STRAIGHT

You have the wind at your back and the uphaul line in your hands. The sail is fluttering at right angles to the board. With your forward foot just in front of the mast and your back foot over the daggerboard, you are ready to get underway. If the front of the board is to your right, your right hand will be the mast hand. The mast hand will be closest to the mast while you're sailing.

Cross your right hand over your left and grab the boom about five inches behind the mast. Pull the mast toward you and tilt it forward until it's in front of your shoulder. With your sail hand (left hand), grasp the boom about three feet from the mast hand. Gradually pull the back of the sail toward you until it fills with wind. This is known as "sheeting in." You will start to move as soon as the wind grabs the sail.

Remember to keep your back straight. Whatever you do, don't bend forward from the waist. Your mast arm should be bent with your mast hand near the shoulder and your sail arm should be almost straight. Bend your knees slightly. To sail straight ahead, keep the mast tilted slightly forward and the boom horizontal.

As you skim along, keep your movements slow and smooth

so you can keep your balance. Jerky moves will end in a dunking! To continue on a straight course, pull the boom toward you with the sail hand only enough to stop the sail from fluttering. Beginners tend to let go of the mast hand when the wind pressure increases. Don't do it! Let out the sail hand and you'll probably be able to get control again without losing your balance.

If the wind gusts are so great that you're being pulled forward, let the sail move away from you or let go with your sail hand completely. The pressure will ease immediately. You will quickly learn how to balance your weight against the force of the wind. As long as you keep the boom parallel to the water and the mast tipped slightly forward, your direction will be straight ahead. Remember, the mast hand steers while the sail hand controls the wind power.

In stronger winds, be sure to keep the mast arm well bent while you ease the sail hand. If the wind suddenly stops, pull in the sail sharply.

If you've tired and want to stop, ease the sail out slowly with your sail hand. As the pressure decreases, hold the rig with your mast hand on the boom or by the uphaul line. Just let the sail flutter until you're ready to get underway again.

To Get Underway

1. Hold the uphaul line while the sail flutters at right angles to the board.

2. Cross your mast hand over and grab the boom.

3. Pull the mast past your shoulder toward the front of the board.

4. Grasp the boom with your sail hand.

5. Slowly pull the sail toward you.

FALLING

If you understand that falling is part of learning, you will learn quickly and have a good time as well. If you absolutely hate to get wet, better stick to checkers or monopoly.

Many beginners automatically let go of their mast hand when hit with the first strong gust of wind. That's a sure way to be pulled off balance. Make it a habit to release the sail hand. If it's impossible to hold on, try to drop both hands at once.

Always make it a point to fall on the opposite side of the sail. Push off with your feet, jump in or just drop backwards into the water. That way you won't hurt yourself or the rig. If you should come up under the sail, just put your hands over your head and work your way to the edge. A deep dive is unnecessary and tiring.

Don't rush to climb back on and haul up the sail. Take your time. Sit a moment on the board and think through the steps to get underway. Relax. You balance more easily when you're not all tensed up. Besides, tension takes away energy you need for windsurfing.

TURNING

After you've learned how to sail straight ahead, you'll want to know how to turn. You will then be able to make slow or fast changes in direction and have more control over your sailing. A sailboard can be steered with great accuracy. That is good to know when a brisk breeze is pushing you straight for a pile of rocks.

To turn into the wind, tilt the mast toward the back of the board and shift your weight to the back foot. If you want to turn your bow away from the wind, lean the mast toward the front of the board. At the same time shift some of your weight to your front leg. As your craft responds to the wind, you'll soon get the feel of how far to tilt the mast. The best way to learn turning is to practice sailing a zigzag course.

A complete turning into the wind is called coming about or tacking. Lean the mast toward the rear of the board and put most of your weight on the rear foot. Release your sail hand first, then the mast hand. Take hold of the uphaul line and as the board turns, walk around the mast in small shuffling steps. Your feet should be close to the mast. Keep the rig in front of you. Let the sail swing over the back of the board to the other side. Remember to keep your back straight and your legs as relaxed as possible.

Once you're completely around on the other side, begin just as you did when you were starting out. Your mast hand will now

become the sail hand. The sail should be at right angles to the board. Cross one hand over, grab the boom and tip the mast toward the front of the board. Pull the boom in with your sail hand until you feel the pressure of the wind. Now you are sailing in the opposite direction from which you came.

Turning away from the wind is called jibing. Lean the mast toward the bow and shift your weight to the front foot. Let go of the boom with the sail hand and catch hold of the uphaul line. Swing the sail over the bow to the other side. You will be facing the front of the board with your feet behind the mast. Continue to swing the sail around until you are back in the starting position. Wait to grab the boom until the sail is at right angles to the board. Don't worry if your board stops entirely or even drifts backward.

When turning has become an automatic process, your turns will be much less jerky. Instead of turning the board around while the sail flutters, you'll sail around in an arc, keeping wind in the sail most of the way. When tacking and jibing come naturally, the sail will only flutter briefly as you use the board's forward motion to swing your craft smoothly around.

CHAPTER 10

RACING
and other
COMPETITIVE CHALLENGES

Sailboard racing began as soon as the second sailboard was made. While windsurfing is great fun as a solo sport, many find the challenge of outsailing someone else irresistible.

Racing gives you a chance to test your ability against others. You will also see what experts can do on a sailboard. Your craft is capable of amazing things!

Racing takes total concentration. Decisions have to be made quickly. Your wits as well as your strength will be tested on every leg of the course.

Boardsailors who race learn to sharpen their skills, but there are plenty of other rewards. You will enjoy traveling to different areas. Boardsailors are usually active, outgoing people who share your love of the outdoors. New friends are easily made when everyone has so much in common. Where else can you find a whole crowd of people who get a thrill from grabbing the wind and running with it?

Race divisions are determined by weight. Since lighter people usually have an advantage, serious sailors watch their diets carefully. Of course your level of fitness will make a real difference

in your performance. In windsurfing nearly every muscle in your body is active. Since fingers and forearms tend to become tired over a long haul, you may want to do some exercises. Pull-ups will help, as will squeezing a spring-loaded hand exerciser or a rubber ball.

Knowing the rules well can make all the difference. Boardsailors are usually under the rules of the International Yacht Racing Union as well as those for each individual class. It will pay to study the special instructions for each event.

One of the toughest windsurfing races is the San Francisco Bay Crossing. Boardsailors must deal with tricky winds, waves and currents, cold water and the hazards of shipping traffic. No wonder usually less than half of those who start are able to finish.

The ad for one Bay race said it all:

Wanted: Young (under 70), Brave (Stupid?), Strong Windsurfer Sailors for a Long, Perilous Journey across the Golden Gate of San Francisco! (Orphans preferred)

Sailboard racing is a fast growing new sport. It is now an international sport with district, national and international championships. The International Yacht Racing Union has recognized the sailboard as an official "International Class" and declared boardsailing an Olympic sport beginning in 1984.

In addition to traditional triangular course events, there are a number of other competitions. Team racing, in which the total position of three boardsailors is all important, is popular. Slalom courses, much like slalom races for skiers, test the competitor's speed and agility. Sailors first head toward the wind, tacking around each buoy. When they reach the top of the course, they cross over to a second line of buoys and then run downwind jibing around each one in turn.

Surf-sailing races offer a chance to match your skills against winds and waves as well as other sailors. If you have the timing of a trapeze artist and can zip your board in and out of the breaking surf, you may find this an interesting way to spend an afternoon.

Buoyball is attracting attention. This team sport is a water version of soccer or polo. Two teams of four sailors each try to

get a large ball (with a handle attached) past the other team. Five points are awarded for sailing over the goal with the ball, three points for throwing it through. Sails must be kept out of the water while the ball is being picked up, and the opponent may only "tackle" the one with the ball when they're both on the same tack. Needless to say, you must be able to change direction swiftly. It's a terrific spectator sport. Players find it wildly exciting, too.

Perhaps the most interesting contests to watch are the freestyle competitions. A panel of judges scores each boardsailor on a series of unusual moves. The idea is to perform as many different tricks as possible. Contestants sail backward, sitting or lying down. They do deep water starts and then dip their heads, noses, bottoms and/or entire bodies. They demonstrate nose and tail sinks, pirouettes and 360 degree turns called helicopters. If the wind and waves cooperate, some even skim along standing or sitting on the edge of the board. This difficult balancing act is known as rail riding. Somewhere right now one of these windsurfing hotdoggers is cooking up a new trick.

Windsurfing is a fast-moving sport!

GLOSSARY

AFT
Toward the rear or back of the board.

BEAUFORT WIND SCALE
Scale of wind strength and sea conditions classified from Force 0 to Force 12; named for Sir Francis Beaufort, the British admiral who invented it.

BOARDSAILING
Sport in which you skim across the water by controlling a sail while standing on a surfboard-like craft; windsurfing.

BOARDSAILOR
One who windsurfs or boardsails.

BOOM
Part of rig held by boardsailor and used to steer (see **WISHBONE BOOM**).

BOW
Front of sailboard or boat.

CENTERLINE
Imaginary line down the center of the sailboard.

COMING ABOUT
Tacking or turning into the wind.

DAGGERBOARD
Board which juts down into the water and keeps the sail board from slipping sideways.

DRIFT
Movement through the water caused by forces of currents or wind.

EASE
Lessening wind pressure on rig by letting out sail.

FORCE
Classification of wind strength by numbers such as Force 1 (light air) or Force 12 (hurricane); see **BEAUFONT WIND SCALE**.

FORWARD

Toward the bow.

FREE-SAIL SYSTEM

First name given to windsurfing by its inventors.

FRESHENING WIND

A wind that is becoming stronger.

GUST

Sudden increase in speed of wind.

GYBING

Jibing

HYPOTHERMIA

Dangerous chilling of the body's core; sometimes fatal.

INTERNATIONAL DISTRESS SIGNAL

Raising and lowering both hands over head; used only in emergencies.

JIBING

Turning around by going away from the wind; gybing.

LEE OR LEEWARD

Side which is away from the wind; downwind side.

MAST

Flexible pole which holds sail on sailboard.

MAST HAND

Hand on the boom which is nearest the mast; forward hand.

NEOPRENE

Rubber material from which wet suits are made (see **WET SUIT**).

OFFSHORE WIND
Wind which blows from land to water.

ONSHORE WIND
Wind which blows from water to land.

POLYETHYLENE
Plastic outer shell of Windsurfer.

POLYURETHANE FOAM
Buoyant but stiff inner core of Windsurfer.

PORT
Left side of board or boat as you face forward.

RAIL
Edge of board.

RIG
Mast, boom and sail of sailboard.

ROCKET
Sailboard designed for experienced boardsailors.

SAILBOARD
Craft consisting of sail, board, mast and booms; used for windsurfing.

SAILBOARDING
Windsurfing; boardsailing.

SAIL HAND
Hand on boom which is farthest from the mast; back hand.

SIMULATOR
Device resembling sailboard or standing area of sailboard used on land to help teach windsurfing.

SHEETING IN
Pulling the sail toward you to increase wind pressure.

SKEG
Small fixed rear fin on underside of sailboard.

STARBOARD
Right side of board or boat as you face forward.

STERN
Rear part of the sailboard.

TACK
Turning into the wind; coming about.

UNIVERSAL JOINT
In sailboards, connects mast to board and allows sail to tilt in any direction.

UPHAUL LINE
Line attached to point where boom meets mast; used to raise sail.

WET SUIT
Rubber suit worn for protection against cold.

WINDSURFER
Sailboard.

WINDSURFING
Sport in which you skim across the water by maneuvering a sail while standing on a surfboard-like craft; boardsailing.

WINDWARD
Side nearest the wind; upwind side.

WISHBONE BOOM
Double boom shaped like a wishbone which extends sail and is used by boardsailor to steer.

Books available through Survival Medical Outfitters, P.O. Box 10102, Merrillville, Indiana 46410. Check, money order, VISA, and Mastercard accepted; please include expiration date of card. Write or call (219) 769-0585.

Commercial orders must be addressed to Stackpole Books, P.O. Box 1831, Cameron and Kelker Streets, Harrisburg, Pennsylvania 17105. For fast service use the toll free number. Call 1-800-READ NOW. For library telemarketing orders, call 1-800-LIBRARI. In Pennsylvania, call (717) 234-5041. Please call between 8:30 a.m. and 4:00 p.m. EST.

WILDERNESS MEDICINE
William W. Forgey, M.D.
An informative medical procedures manual written specifically for outdoorsmen interested in preventing, diagnosing and treating common illnesses and injuries. Emergency medical and surgical techniques are described in simple terms. Devoted to the selection of medications, both prescription and non-prescription and their use under wilderness conditions. **Paperback**, 5½ x 8½, 120 pages, photos, diagrams, illus. 0-934802-14-9 **$9.95** Canadian $12.95

"... a clear, concise guide to treating the gamut of outdoor mishaps, from insect bites and fishhook removal to more serious problems such as broken bones and heatstroke."
Sports Afield 11/84

HYPOTHERMIA - Death by Exposure
by William W. Forgey, M.D.
Hypothermia is the lowering of the body's core temperature to the point that illness and death can result. It can be prevented. It can be treated. But only if you know how. Hypothermia is the greatest potential danger for anyone traveling in the outdoors -- whether fishing, hunting, camping, climbing, or even driving down an Interstate Highway. Outdoors medical expert, Dr. William Forgey, explores the causes, methods of prevention, advances in clothing, field treatments, hospital care, and the basics of physiology and physics of hypothermia in terms everyone can understand. Paperback, , 6x9, 172 pages, illus., index, glossary, bibliography.
ISBN 0-934802-10-6 **$9.95** Canadian $12.95

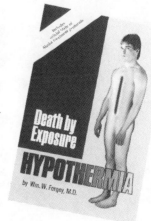

CANOEING WILD RIVERS
Cliff Jacobson

An easy reading manual, of source material, canoeing tips, advanced techniques, and gear recommendations by a weathered expert. **Paperback**, 340 pages, color photos, illus.

0-934802-17-3 **$14.95** Canadian 17.95

"If you've ever dreamed of canoeing Alaska's arctic rivers, or for that matter, any waterway in North America, then **Canoeing Wild Rivers** *is the first book you should obtain."*

Alaska Outoors 11/84

"This book, **Canoeing Wild Rivers,** *by Cliff Jacobson is the one I recommend above all others ... It is not a re-hash of previous writers, but the accumulated learnings of much personal experience."*

Verlen Kruger ['84]
Ultimate Canoe Challenge member

HIKING
Calvin Rutstrum

A comprehensive, procedural coverage from the short urban walk to the extensive wilderness trek, with analysis of equipment, outdoor living methods, and modern hiking ethics. **Paperback**, 6x9, 125 pages, photos, illus.

0-934802-20-3 **$8.95** Canadian $11.95

BACK COUNTRY
Calvin Rutstrum

A volume of adventures, trips and events from the Northern Wilderness during the first part of this century. **Paperback**, 6x9, 255 pages, Les Kouba illus.

0-934802-11-4 **$14.95** Canadian $17.95

COOKING THE DUTCH OVEN WAY
Woody Woodruff
Written by a designer/manufacturer of dutch ovens, and a 50-year Scouter and life-long camper and hiker. Recipes for good old fashioned dishes and baker's favorites, easily prepared at home or in the north-woods. **Paperback**, 6x9, 142 pages, illus.
0-934802-01-7 **$8.95** Canadian $11.95

COOKING THE WILD HARVEST
J. Wayne Fears
Over 250 recipes recommended by various agri-cultural universities' Cooperative Extension Service home economists. Fears combines his talents as a wildlife biologist, outdoorsman, and prize-winning outdoor writer for hints on proper field dressing and procuring. **Paperback**, 6x9, 185 pages.
0-934802-14-9 **$12.95** Canadian $15.95

HODIO
C.N. Day
The true story of a 19-year-old American seaman cap-tured off the shores of Burma during a naval battle of World War II. For the 42 months in brutal prison camps of Indonesia, **HODIO** became synonymous with Prisoner of War. **Paperback**, 5½ x 8½, 216 pages.
0-934802-13-0 **$9.95** Canadian $12.95

A TRAPPER'S LEGACY
Carl Schels

A rare glimpse of a professional trapper's life, difficulties, and dangers of existence deep in the wilderness. Forced into poverty by the Great Depression, Carl Schels decided to chase his dream of wilderness living and survived to write this story -- his legacy. **Paperback**, 5½ x 8½, 212 pages, photos. 0-934802-12-2 **$9.95** Canadian $12.95

THE BEGINNING BOWHUNTER
Tony Kinton

A thorough examination of equipment, techniques, and hunting applications of the modern bow. Illustrated and written by a professional hunter and writer who covers all aspects of this sport. The perfect book for someone wanting the latest information on equipment available and how to use it. Methods of target practice and hunting skills included. **Paperback**, 6x9, 144 pages, photos, illustrations, index.
0-934802-21-1 **$9.95** Canadian $12.95

WINDSURFING
Diana Gleasner

Sailboards can bring the excitement of surfboards to water anywhere. Even a light breeze can turn a small pond into a surfing adventure. **WINDSURFING** is a complete guide to the use, care, and safety precautions for the beginning sailboarder. Careful explanations and photographs illustrate all aspects of this exciting sport. **Paperback**, 6x9, 120 pages, photos, index, glossary.
0-934802-24-6 **$7.95** Canadian $9.95

ICEFISHING - Methods and Magic
Steven A. Griffin

Fishing enthusiasts do not have to stop fishing after the first snowfall. In fact, real enthusiasts find the most generous fishing holes during the most beautiful and quiet time of the year -- the winter. Well illustrated, this book of winter fishing techniques shows how to eliminate discomfort and maximize your fishing.

6x9, 144 pages, photos, index.
0-934802-25-4 **$9.95** Canadian $12.95